9/15

POWERING UP A CAREER IN ROBOTICS

PETER K. RYAN

ROSEN
PUBLISHING®

New York

Published in 2016 by The Rosen Publishing Group, Inc.
29 East 21st Street, New York, NY 10010

Copyright © 2016 by The Rosen Publishing Group, Inc.

First Edition

Library of Congress Cataloging-in-Publication Data

Ryan, Peter K., author.
Powering up a career in robotics Peter K. Ryan.—First edition.
    pages cm.—(Preparing for tomorrow's careers)
 Includes bibliographical references and index.
 ISBN 978-1-4994-6085-8 (library bound)
 1. Robotics–Vocational guidance–Juvenile literature. [1. Vocational
guidance.] I. Title.
 TJ211.25.R93 2016
 629.8'92—dc23

                                                    2014046342

Manufactured in the United States of America

CONTENTS

INTRODUCTION

Robots are part of our everyday lives, and most of the time you wouldn't even know it. Robots and robotics are involved in every industry you can think of, and they are part of nearly every product you purchase. Robots build cars, computers, cell phones, televisions, and even clothing. Robotics are involved in the preparation and packaging of foods, in transportation, and in storage and delivery systems. Without being aware of it, we are surrounded by robots that work to make our lives better.

When we talk about robots and robotics, we aren't talking about the futuristic imaginings of science fiction. Rather, we are talking about machines that perform automated tasks for specific purposes. Steadily we are seeing the introduction of robots that are more autonomous and task-specific, such as the iRobot Roomba, a robotic vacuum cleaner that can vacu-

Doctors use a robot to disinfect a room that had housed a patient with the highly infectious disease Ebola. Robots are able to enter hazardous areas that would harm people.

um your entire house on its own. There are robotic assembly plants that make cars from start to finish in less than a single day, with minimal human intervention.

One of the more mundane robots that you encounter is the elevator. Elevators safely carry passengers up and down buildings twenty-four hours a day, seven days a week, 365 days a year. Inside a modern elevator are computer circuits, mechanical actuators, mechanical doors, electric motors, automatic breaks, motion sensors, weight sensors, and more. All of these systems combine to make riding an elevator a completely safe and boring experience. However, one hundred years ago an elevator would have seemed a thing of pure magic and wonder.

Our civilization has fully embraced the use of robotics and robots as tools that help improve our lives and expand our capabilities beyond our own bodies. Robotics has allowed humans to explore the deepest depths of the oceans, where water pressure is so great that it would crush any submersible carrying human passengers. Robotics has allowed scientists to explore the depths of volcanoes, where gases and high temperatures would instantly kill any person. Robotics has enabled humankind to leave our planet and explore the planets in our solar system without risk to human astronauts.

Behind all of these wonderful machines that make our lives easier and better are the people who work in robotics. For every robot you can think of there is someone who conceived of it, someone who built it, someone who sold it, and someone who maintains it. Those people have careers in robotics, and we are going to discuss how you, too, can make your own path toward your very own career in robotics.

The future of robotics and robots is very bright and exciting. For those young people who decide to pursue careers in robotics there will be a future of choice and opportunity. Young roboticists will get to invent the science fiction imaginings of today in the real products of tomorrow. As our combined technological capabilities continue to increase so will the number of jobs and opportunities for those who work in robotics.

So now is the time for you, young reader, to power up your future career in robotics!

CHAPTER ONE

ROBOTS ON THE RISE!

One of the most discussed robotic devices in use today is the military drone, a medium-sized, unmanned aircraft that can be sent anywhere in the world to conduct aerial military operations. Military drones are not autonomous, meaning they don't operate without the control of a human operator. However, many of the most simple and common tasks a flying drone performs are automated. A drone can take off and land, fly to a designated area, and return home all without the intervention of a human pilot. Drones are programmed with capabilities that reduce the workload of the drone operators so that they can focus on the specific tasks they are assigned.

Another type of drone that we are all very familiar with is the commercial airplane.

Members of the U.S. Air Force prepare to launch a small reconnaissance drone during a training exercise. Drones and other robots have become standard equipment used by all branches of the U.S. military.

Modern airplanes have very sophisticated autopiloting capabilities that allow the plane to take off, fly, and land in a predetermined location without intervention from a pilot. We don't think of airplanes as robotic, but inside each airplane there are sophisticated computers, actuators, servos, and other mechanical parts all operated for the purpose of safe flight. So essentially a modern airplane is a robot, so to speak.

ATLAS

Atlas is a robot designed and manufactured by a company called Boston Dynamics. It is a 6-foot, 330-pound (1.8-meter, 150-kilogram) two-legged and two-armed robot. It has many sensors and computer components to allow it to walk independently, carry objects, analyze its surroundings and interact with its environment.

Atlas was partially funded by DARPA (Defense Advance Research Projects Agency) for the DARPA Robotic Challenge, a multiteam competition designed to bring companies and universities together to complete complex challenges for robots, such as climbing ladders, navigating obstacles, and opening doors. Atlas is one of the most advanced robots ever developed in the United States. Its intended purpose is to access highly hazardous areas, like that of a nuclear accident, for information gathering and potential search-and-rescue operations.

SCIENCE FICTION VS. REALITY

When discussing robotics, it is important to understand that the depictions in movies and on television are not always realistic and that robotics are in fact quite common. Take the robotic assemblers at a car manufacturing plant. There are hundreds of independent robotic devices. Each has specific capabilities and tasks that all work together to assemble a large number of parts into a finished car. Parts and pieces of cars get moved through an automated assembly line where robots weld, bolt, fasten, paint, and assemble the parts to create a fully functioning car.

In large shipping warehouses, robotics can be found moving products, placing products into and out of shelving, identifying items, and gathering items in order to satisfy purchases. Amazon.com is one retail company that relies very heavily on robotic warehouse machines in its order-fulfillment process. When a customer orders an item, the order is fed through Amazon's computer system, which routes the order to the nearest warehouse that stocks the item purchased. From that point a series of robots will assist warehouse employees to locate, collect, pack, and ship the item purchased.

Amazon.com uses robots in its warehouses to gather books and other items for processing, packaging, and delivery. Robots help speed up the entire order-fulfillment process and reduce Amazon's overall warehouse costs.

IT'S ONLY JUST THE BEGINNING!

Despite the incredible levels of automation that we have achieved, we are today only at the very beginning of the robotics revolution. The first use of robotic automated processes in manufacturing appeared in the 1980s. Since that time the sophistication and capabilities of robotics have been staggering. Robots are faster, smaller, cheaper, and smarter.

ASIMO

Created by the special research division of the car company Honda, ASIMO can be considered the most advanced and sophisticated robot ever created. ASIMO can converse with people, walk, run, climb stairs, and perform complex tasks all without any human intervention.

ASIMO has many sensors, including ones in its fingers that allow it to grasp objects firmly and gently based on the feeling, just like people can. ASIMO is capable of pouring coffee from a jar into a paper cup without spilling the coffee or crushing the cup.

The primary purpose for ASIMO is research and development, learning how to improve its capabilities so that one day similar robots can be sold to the public as assistants or companions.

There will be huge leaps in capability and cost that will make robotics available to everyone on the planet. In order to get to that point, young people need to involve themselves in the field of study and build careers in the field. One of the most exciting reasons to get into robotics is that it is field that is still wide open for huge discoveries and breakthroughs. There are many opportunities to be found in the robotics field.

ROBOTS IN SPACE

The cutting edge of robotics development and usage can be found at NASA (National Aeronautics and Space Administration). NASA currently has two rovers operating on the surface of Mars, Opportunity and Curiosity. At the time of this writing, both are collecting data and material samples in order to expand our knowledge about the planet. These rovers represent some of the most complex and sophisticated technical challenges that engineers have ever faced and solved. The rovers flew millions of miles from our planet, entered Mars's orbit, and safely landed within a few feet of their intended targets.

The Mars rovers move about the surface of Mars collecting rock and soil samples, gathering atmospheric data, and searching for anything that may lead to greater discovery about the planet. The rovers utilize sophisticated sensory equipment in order to gather information. Six large wheels provide locomotion, each one delivering power for movement. There are robotic arms for gathering rocks and other materials. There is a micro laboratory on board that can break down

Without the Mars rovers, scientists wouldn't know nearly as much as they do about the red planet. These robots have gathered a wealth of information over the past several years, a feat no human could have accomplished.

materials and study their component parts. There is a sophisticated communications relay system that allows for transmission of radio signals back to Earth.

In 2003, the Japan Aerospace Exploration Agency launched the Hayabusa mission, which sent an unmanned space vessel to meet an asteroid that would pass near Earth in 2005. The craft was successfully able to intercept its target, land safely, take off, and return to Earth with samples from the asteroid. To put this in context, this is like shooting a bullet at a fired cannonball and not only hitting it but then returning the bullet back to the gun. Truly staggering is the precision of the mathematics in calculating the flight path of the asteroid and the intercept course that was required to land safely. There were teams of engineers and mathematicians working on this project, and because of their collaboration, the mission was a success.

CHAPTER TWO

GETTING STARTED WITH EDUCATION

For the student interested in pursuing a career in the field of robotics, it is important to first understand that robotics consists of many fields of study that are tied together. Every discipline in the fields of science and engineering is utilized in some capacity within robotics. So if you are interested in studying particular fields, such as electronics, but you want to work in robotics, you can do that. The question is, how do you prepare for the path that you need to take in order to be able to do that kind of work?

Within the field of robotics there are many subspecialties that are interrelated and interdependent. Math, engineering, mechanics, materials, and other disciplines are called upon for the creation of nearly every robotic device ever made. Typically the development of a robot requires the skills and input of a team of people, with each member of

ts interested in robotics will likely
o study complex mathematics such
anced algebra and calculus.

ROBOT CAMPS

Throughout the nation there are summer camps that students of all ages can attend to gain first-hand experience designing, building, and programming robots. A great example of the kinds of programs that students can participate in is iD Tech. There are programs designed for different age ranges with increasing complexity toward the older groups. Students work in teams with mentors and teachers on projects to create robotic solutions to a variety of different types of problems. Students also have classroom training on the tools and technologies that are employed in their program.

For younger students the projects are simpler but still require patience, hard work, and ingenuity. Systems like LEGO Mindstorms are used to make the building and programming somewhat easy. Older students are set to work on sophisticated robotics parts from companies like VEX, which require tools and mechanical know-how to assemble and operate.

Robot camps are a great way to get first-hand exposure to working with robots, working in teams, and meeting other students who are also interested in robotics.

the team bringing a specialty or expertise to the effort. This is critical to the field of robotics. The depth of expertise required within each discipline is too great for one individual alone. It is not possible for one person to be an expert in enough fields to accomplish what a team of field experts can do together.

FOLLOW YOUR INSTINCTS

During your time in grammar school and high school you will be exposed to many of the fields of scientific study in your various science classes. It is important that you participate fully in each of these different classes so that you can learn the material and discover what interests you and what doesn't. If you find that you love biology but not physics, you can still pursue a career in robotics. And now you know that your path will probably be more enjoyable if you focus on biology and its application in robotics.

The same is true of all science and math disciplines. If you love math but not biology, you can still be involved in robotics. The trick to finding your path is to jump headfirst into lots of different areas of study. Give each one your best effort to see if it's the right field for you.

It must be said that in order to truly consider a career in any scientific field, one must work very hard in the basic areas of science and math. The basics include algebra, geometry, trigonometry, calculus, biology, physics, and chemistry, all of which can be studied in grammar school and high school. The best way to prepare for a

Chemistry and the other basic sciences are the foundation of any career in robotics. Chemistry is critical to developing new materials for robotics to be made lighter, faster, and more durable.

career in science is to truly apply yourself to the basic fields of science as soon as you can and develop mastery of the basic concepts. Slowly over time you will develop strong skills that will prepare you for college-level study.

Before you get into college, you do have to get through the daunting task of taking college entrance exams and possibly other aptitude tests required by your

LEGO MINDSTORMS AND FIRST LEGO LEAGUE

LEGO Mindstorms are a product category produced and manufactured by the Danish company LEGO, the maker of the assembly toys since 1949. Mindstorms are made of highly complex parts, servos, motors, and controllers that interface with computers.

Mindstorm sets allow for the creation of animated robotics that are programmable for any purpose the creator chooses. The kits come with programmable interfaces and with connectors allowing for complex programmability on a computer. LEGO offers free software for download to both PCs and Macs.

The First LEGO League (FLL) is a LEGO-sponsored camp for kids up to age sixteen. Members work with LEGO Mindstorm kits to solve complex tasks and problems in a team setting. The camp lasts about a week, exposing students to full-time LEGO employees and giving them an opportunity to gain professional experience during their time with LEGO.

state or school district. Preparing for these exams may seem pointless. However, the concepts and skills you must master in order to succeed at the tests are founded entirely on the subjects you must study during school.

Many top schools base their enrollment on your performance on these standardized tests. This process can seem unfair to those who don't test well, but unfortunately that is the system that is in place. The best way to deal with these exams is to start preparing for them as soon as possible. You can go to any bookstore (in person or online) and purchase SAT or ACT preparation books.

STEM

The STEM curriculum (science, technology, engineering, and math) has recently been challenged by many educators. Some are now fighting to redesign the curriculum to STEAM (science, technology, engineering, arts, and math). The study of the arts helps to create depth and substance. It allows students to connect with the deep questions of life and to instill a sense of belonging in the world, which is often overlooked in the pursuit of basic scientific education.

Great scientific thinkers and discoverers have always been balanced in their pursuit of science with their pursuit of the arts. Leonardo da Vinci was not only one of the most brilliant scientists of his time but also among the greatest artists. Benjamin Franklin was not only an inventor but also a master politician and strategist.

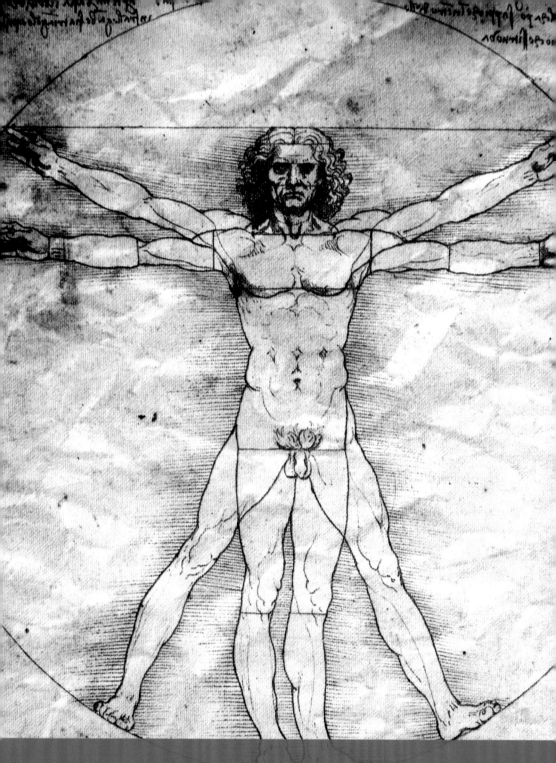

Leonardo da Vinci's *Vitruvian Man* represents the union of art and science, an ideal that many in the field of robotics strive for.

"EXTRA CREDIT"

Beyond classroom study there are many opportunities for you to get involved with robotics in a hands-on way. There are robotics clubs, robotics programs, and the Internet, which holds unlimited amounts of information to help you get started on your very own robotics projects. Maybe you are interested in photography and want to experiment with taking video from a quadcopter drone, but you want to build the copter on your own. Perhaps you are interested in marine life and want to take photos of undersea creatures without having to dive down, so you build a submersible drone to take photos for you. Perhaps your plans involve something more practical, like developing a device that will turn your house lights on when the day turns into night. There are an unlimited number of projects you can take on yourself and complete with a little research, help, and hard work.

CHAPTER THREE

THE WORLD OF ENGINEERING

The fields of engineering are numerous. The most commonly found engineering degree programs are electrical, mechanical, computer, chemical, and civil engineering. Each area of study is highly specialized, but there are always some areas of overlap between each field. At the most basic level, mathematics, physics, chemistry, and biology all intersect in the study of any of the fields of engineering. However as one progresses deeper into each field of study, the level of specialization that is reached increases greatly.

Depending upon the intended application of a particular robotics project, different types of engineering skills will be called upon. If the project is going to be creating an autonomous biped then it is logical that electrical, mechanical, and computer engineers will be highly utilized. In the case of a surgical robot that will assist surgeons in microsurgeries, it is likely that biomechanical engineers will be required.

Surgeons rely heavily on robotic surgical tools to achieve levels of precision and detail impossible with the human hand and eye alone.

TEAMWORK IN ENGINEERING

Engineering specialization is absolutely critical because of the limitless depth of knowledge that one can study in any given field of engineering. When engineers with different expertise collaborate, wonderful things can be made. Consider the NASA Apollo program, when the United States sent astronauts to the moon. Every single conceivable engineering field was utilized for the project. There were hundreds of engineers who collaborated on the project, and the end result was the successful delivery of men safely to the moon and back.

More recently, Google has undertaken a project of creating an autonomous car. This project has been the effort of hundreds of engineers across the fields of electrical, computer, and civil engineering. In addition to the project team that built the autonomous cars were many thousands of computer engineers and cartographers who collaborated on the creation of massive and highly precise global mapping systems. These systems are

The future of the automobile will surely incorporate robotics. The Google Car is the result of many years of effort by a large team of robotics and computer engineers at Google.

a major underpinning of the Google self-driving car project. The effort could not have succeeded without the initial work undertaken during the creation of Google Maps.

MECHANICAL ENGINEERING

Mechanical engineers, as the name implies, study the mechanical world of things. They use physics and mathematics to study materials, motion, and scientific laws to create incredible devices. A mechanical engineer will be able to tell you very precisely the nature of an object's probable path of travel given its design and where it is traveling. Mechanical engineers working in the field of robotics are most commonly found designing locomotion and articulation.

Students pursuing a degree or career in mechanical engineering should have strong mathematics skills and a natural inclination toward understanding how things work. In the field of robotics, mechanical engineers are highly valued because they are the people who design the structures, the legs, the wheels, the arms, the housings, and any other physical elements that make up a robotic device.

Mechanical engineers study in great detail how well a system works and then optimize that design and system. In the case of iRobot's Roomba robotic vacuum, the mechanical engineers are responsible for selecting the materials chosen for the product. They also design the manufacturing process that creates the parts and design the assembly process that sees all the parts integrated into the final device. The mechanical engineer works hand in hand with designers and turns the concept into reality by applying practical capability to design goals.

UNDERGRADUATE DEGREE IN ROBOTICS ENGINEERING AT WPI

Worcester Polytechnic Institute (WPI) offers one of the best robotics engineering programs in the world. Students complete a four-year program that includes classes in mathematics, basic science, mechanics, electronics, computer science, and more.

The program and degree are multidisciplinary because they require students to master skills across different degree types. Students are required to work on team projects throughout the program that result in the production of robotics designed for specific tasks and functions.

The WPI robotics engineering department also sponsors a team to participate in the DARPA Robotics Challenge. During the most recent robotics challenge, WPI teamed with students from Carnegie Mellon University (CMU) to compete. Their entrance was made using the ATLAS robot from Boston Dynamics.

COMPUTER ENGINEERING

Computer engineers study an area that intersects computer science and electrical engineering. Most often, computer engineers design and build the components that computers are made of, design computer systems, or work to optimize existing computer software. The difference between computer engineering and computer science is that computer scientists develop computer code or theoretical aspects of computer programming. Computer engineers work with the physical processors, circuits, and chips that make up a computer along with the code that will allow it to operate.

Computer engineers are critical to the field of robotics because the software they develop enables the inanimate device to become a robotic device. Computer engineers work

Robotics requires knowledge of computer coding. Students who compete in robotics competitions can develop new coding and software skills while having a bit of fun.

closely with mechanical and electrical engineers to create the systems that control the sensory, locomotion, and articulation functions of the robotic device.

Any student interested in computer engineering should have a strong passion and inclination for working with computer code and computer equipment. This is a field of study well suited to those students who, for example, like to take a cell phone apart in order to hack in a new battery or better Wi-Fi chip.

In addition to possessing a strong liking for computers, the student pursuing a degree or career in computer engineering must also have strong skills in mathematics, physics, and chemistry. Mathematics is the base layer of all computer technology. Physics dictates the behavior of electrons as they pass through circuitry. Chemistry is fundamental to understanding what materials must be used in computer design in order to achieve optimal computer operation.

ELECTRICAL ENGINEERING

Electrical engineers study electricity and all the ways it can be harnessed for human use. Our entire history of computer and robotic development was built on the shoulders of electrical engineering. This field studies the flow of current and how it can be manipulated across many different scales of applications.

Some electrical engineers learn how to deal with very large electrical systems like a power grid where millions of volts of current flow to feed our homes, schools, and businesses. Some electrical engineers study the very small application of electricity on things like transistors, capacitors, and circuitry. In any area of focus an electrical engineer relies very heavily on mathematics, physics, and chemistry.

In the case of robotics, the electrical engineer will design the electrical systems that transport and store power for use by the robotic device. The electrical engineer will work in tandem with the mechanical engineer to help determine the types of motors and batteries employed on a project to achieve specific goals. The electrical engineer will work with the computer engineer to ensure that the computers on the robotic device receive enough power

Complex control centers, such as this one at an electrical power grid, use robotic sensors, controls, and actuators to safely maintain operations.

and electrical shielding to ensure their successful operation.

CHEMICAL ENGINEERING

Chemical engineers study the physical properties of matter. The title of the field of study is a bit misleading because it implies it is the study of chemistry, which we all know is the study of interactions of chemicals. However, chemicals make up the entire natural world that we can see and interact with, and every chemical interacts with every other chemical differently. Chemical engineering is the study of the fundamental interactions of all chemicals.

One of the most important roles that chemical engineers play, relative to robotics, is material design and analysis. A chemical engineer on a robotics project will help determine what kinds of materials should be used in the making of the device in order to achieve targeted goals.

Any student interested in pursuing chemical engineering should possess strong mathematics skills, pursue classes in chemistry and physics, and be very interested in the study of the periodic table of elements. A degree in chemical engineering is considered by most engineers to be the most difficult to achieve because of the intensity of the mathematics and volume of material that must be memorized.

CHAPTER FOUR

ROBOTICS DESIGN

A present-day example of a creative designer who drives engineering output is Jony Ive, the chief product designer at Apple. Ive is the man responsible for the design of nearly every piece of hardware that consumers have purchased from Apple since the introduction of the very first Apple iPod. Many consider Ive to be a genius because his designs are both highly functional and have a beautiful aesthetic, which in and of itself makes his devices beautiful. The marriage of the functional with the beautiful is an approach to design that dates back as far as the Greek empire. Then, the first engineers were building the acropolis and chose to create beauti-

Researchers can even create robotic animals. Learning about the mechanics of animal movement teaches scientists how to improve robotic mobility.

33

ful marble columns. These were not only stunning to behold, but they could also support enormous weight. They inspired new kinds of structures to be built.

The term "designer" is quite vague and can imply a wide range of different skill sets, roles, and careers. However, because we live in an age of job specialization and expertise, the type of design one will perform will depend upon the kind of skills developed during one's education and professional life. The type of design one will do also depends upon the natural inclinations and interests of the individual. Some students may be interested in the field of transportation while others may be interested in the field of communications. These two students will develop different sensibilities about design and how it should be applied to their specific projects and fields of interest.

FORM VS. FUNCTION

Industrial designers constantly struggle to balance form and function. Form describes the appearance and aesthetic appeal of a product. Is the device attractive, does it appeal to one's senses? "Function" is a term used to describe how well a device performs its intended purpose. A dump truck is a very purposeful vehicle; it is designed to haul heavy loads of dirt, debris, or refuse. A dump truck is designed to function very well, but it is not designed to be attractive or pleasing to the eye.

Form and function should be complementary, and they play a huge role in the design of robots. ASIMO is a small robot that has little external protection. It is designed to assist with simple civilian tasks like fetching food and greeting visitors.

Atlas is encaged in tubular steel and has the strength to lift very heavy objects and traverse very rugged terrain. All of Atlas's wires, servos, and pneumatics are exposed to the outside. Atlas was designed to serve in potentially rugged terrain and therefore needs to be able to withstand falls and external conditions, and no consideration was taken for its aesthetic appeal.

If an art student and an engineering student were separately asked to draw a concept for a robot to carry groceries they would likely create two very different designs. The art student would probably design a robot that is very attractive and beautiful. The engineering student would probably design something very practical and serviceable. Neither of these two approaches is right or wrong. They are merely the representations of art and engineering.

INDUSTRIAL DESIGN

The field of industrial design is at its core the study of the impact design has on utility and consumer preference. By applying various levels of aesthetic artistry and balancing the functionality of a product against its aesthetics, it is possible to design a product that is both beautiful and functional. This balancing act between form and function is at the core of the field of industrial design.

Students who pursue a career in industrial design for robotics should have interest in artistry and practical engineering. The industrial designer will work with engineers and other artists to create elements for robotics projects. The value that an industrial designer will bring to the project is his or her innate and trained understanding of product design in the current marketplace. The industrial designer will know what kinds of colors, shapes, and overall look will appeal most to a potential consumer based upon how other products have either succeeded or failed in the marketplace.

USER EXPERIENCE

Another area of design that is critical to the potential success of a robotics project is user experience and usability design. User experience or user interface designers study the interplay between humans and machines. This is to understand what kinds of controls or interfaces best enable the human operator

Students can work with teachers to learn what works and what doesn't when it comes to robot design and user experience.

or create the best experience and sensation of the operator.

This kind of designer may work in the field of computer interfaces or physical controls. The successful user interface designer is one who has supreme attention to detail and sensitivity to colors, shapes, and sounds and how they inform the overall experience of a user.

THE BUSINESS SIDE OF ROBOTICS

As with any commercial effort, there is always a need for business professionals who are responsible for the financing, marketing, sales, and distribution of products. In the field of robotics there are many career paths available for individuals with business skills and training. This is important for any student who may not be interested in engineering or design. The businessperson who works in the field of robotics is critical to the success of a project.

The field of business is quite large, and as with all other areas of study and professional endeavor, it has become highly specialized. The most common types of business careers fall into accounting, finance, operations, management, human resources, and sales.

tele-presence robots, employees work off-site can move the robot see through its "eyes" as if they actually there.

DRONES TO THE RESCUE

Japan sits squarely on top of a major fault line that is a cause of constant earthquakes. In the past, Japan has suffered enormous disasters from major earthquakes and the tsunamis that can be created by earthquakes. As a result of this constant exposure to danger, the Japanese have been aggressively pursuing options to improve how their rescue workers and first responders reach more people faster and more effectively.

One of the major efforts that the Japanese government has fostered is the development of robots that can locate, pick up, and safely transport disaster victims away from immediate threats to safer locations for treatment and care. These robots will likely serve to save many lives in a major disaster.

FINANCE

Finance is a field of study primarily focused on the raising and management of capital for the purpose of funding businesses and projects. Every company engaged in the field of robotics has a financier on its team or in its employ in order to get money to fund its work.

The Roomba is a robotic vacuum cleaner that automatically vacuums a floor without any human interaction. The Roomba uses several sensors and processors to navigate its environment and to sense the dirt on the floor.

In the case of the Roomba, the parent company iRobot had to come up with funding in order to pay for all the designers, engineers, and materials required to build the first prototype. Once the first prototype was built and approved, the company had to raise even more money in order to acquire the manufacturing facility, the raw materials, and the employees to assemble the device.

Once the manufacturing was funded, iRobot needed to fund the marketing campaign to let potential customers know about the product. It also needed the money for the packaging that the Roomba would ship in and for a full-time support and warranty department. All throughout this process, the finance department was critical because it was responsible for ensuring that when money was needed it was available.

For those students interested in finance, their focus should be on the study of mathematics, accounting, operations, and general business. Most of these classes are taught at a basic level in high school and at a very deep level at universities.

OPERATIONS

After the design and engineering is complete and after the prototype has been delivered and the final product approved for assembly, the role of the operations specialist is required. The businessperson who focuses on operations is one who studies the processes and practices required to efficiently manage manufacturing and production.

In the field of robotics, the operations personnel aren't going to design any of the parts or pieces that make up the final product. They are the people who are going to ensure that there are always ample materials to keep the assembly line moving and to ensure that there are always enough staff with proper training to keep the plant operating.

Individuals who work in operations focus very closely on finding the optimum procedures and processes to produce the maximum number of products at the lowest possible cost while maintaining the highest level of quality. The field of study of operations is relatively new, and it is a multidisciplinary field that focuses on mathematics, management, organizational design, and human resources.

For the student interested in operations, focus should be placed on mathematics, accounting, finance, general business, human resources, and psychology. At the high school level, operations is very rarely taught, but a student could gain exposure through summer jobs or internships. At the university level, operations is a subset of the school of business.

MARKETING

Marketing is the name of a whole field of practice revolving around observation, analysis, and communication of the current marketplace for a particular product or category of products. In the field of robotics there are many different industries that are served, so the efforts of the marketing professional will be determined by the target customer or marketplace.

The day-to-day life of a marketer is dependent upon the life cycle of a product or company. If a product is new and is about to go to the marketplace, the role of the marketer is to work with advertisers and sales to help make the product highly visible and appear highly attractive. Once a product has been successfully sold and is established in the marketplace, the marketing professional will study data about sales and trends to find any possible area of incremental sales growth he or she can.

For the student interested in marketing, the focus of study should be on mathematics, statistics, psychology, human behavior, and general business. This career also requires that the student be constantly in touch with current trends, fashions, products, and technologies in order to keep abreast of what consumers are buying and why.

Marketing is sometimes taught at the high school level, however, gaining experience in marketing can be had by participating in student government, fund-raising, or club activities requiring recruitment. At the university level, marketing is a subset of the school of business.

SALES

Sales is a combination of art and science. It is a skill that is both learned and innately possessed. Some salespeople have a natural talent for selling; others have to learn to develop skills to sell. Ultimately the process of selling is about telling a story of value to a potential buyer. The salesperson is responsible for convincing buyers that the product he or she sells will provide value that is equal to or greater than the money required to purchase it. Salespeople sell products or services, and sometimes both. It is the goal of the salesperson to successfully convince a buyer to give money for the product or service he or she is trying to sell.

In the robotics industry there are many sales roles. Because most of the robotics on the market today are designed for industrial applications, the sales jobs available require a fairly extensive technical capability. It is required that sales professionals know the very technical nature of the robotics they sell and that they have a very deep knowledge of their customers' needs.

Preparing for a career path in technical sales requires as much technical education as a typical

Business school students learn the art of delivering business presentations and selling to customers, key skills for success in the robotics industry.

engineering degree. The student who is interested in a career in technical sales should focus his or her study on mathematics, science, psychology, and general business.

At the grammar school and high school levels, sales is rarely taught. However anyone can open a lemonade stand or dog-walking business to gain critical sales experience. At the university level, sales is not a dedicated discipline, but a student can gain ample exposure to engineering and business training for the field of robotics.

Most technical sales roles are not typically available to young people fresh out of college. Technical sales jobs require experience in the professional world and years of maturation. The best way to wind up in a sales role is to become an expert in a technical field and to maintain and develop strong interpersonal skills.

PREPARING FOR A CAREER IN ROBOTICS

Assuming that you are interested in pursuing a particular line of study and work in the field of robotics, it is now time to ask yourself what you can do to start preparing for that future. It may seem like your college days are very far away, but preparing for a career in today's highly competitive career environment requires a very high level of dedication and preparation.

Preparing for a career in robotics will require a lot of hard work. The following are individual steps that should be undertaken collectively in order to give students the best possible chance at getting into a good university program and the career path of their choosing.

HITTING THE BOOKS

The value of working diligently and consistently on academics from now until graduation from university cannot be stressed enough. Students interested in pursuing a career in robotics must understand that they will be competing with students from around the world for a very limited number of jobs. Because the jobs will be limited, the intensity of competition will be

Careers in robotics require a high level of education. Studying hard and getting good grades now will pay off in the future.

great. It is very important that students perform their absolute best in every class and subject at all times.

This can be very challenging because the years during grammar school and high school are some of the most fun. And after all, you are only young once. However students who intend to succeed in the world of robotics must accept that they must work very hard and sacrifice much of their playtime to study time. This is not to say that no fun can be had, but it is very important to balance life so that academic excellence is achieved.

Following the guidance of the STEM curriculum with the addition of arts-based classes will provide a student with ample exposure to the material needed to prepare for college. Pursuing classes in math, computer programming, metalworking, electronics, chemistry, and physics is a great way to gain academic skills that will prepare one for collegiate and professional success in robotics.

CURRICULUM VITAE AND RÉSUMÉ

The curriculum vitae is a summary of academic history and success for an individual. It is often referred to as a CV. All student should prepare a CV, which lists the names of the schools they attend, the classes they take, the academic achievements earned, any scholarships or awards, and the timeframe of all of these items in chronological order. The CV provides a quick snapshot of a student's academic history.

A résumé provides a snapshot of the professional and work achievements of an individual. The information listed on a résumé will include work experience,

01/200

The résumé is the most important tool a job seeker in robotics can use to tell potential employers about his or her interests and experience. A résumé highlights your strengths.

RESUME

Street Name. 1
70000 City Name
Tel: 0000 5555555
E-Mail: emailname@server.com

MARY

erience in commercial engines development
rt knowledge in programming
g experience in software design and architecture, animation, network programming,
nance optimization
s of development experience. Worked on projects in various industries.
ment of a small team of engineers

PERIENCE

nt   Company Name Ltd. (United States)
Lead Position Name

Working on new innovative project

- Sed sed ipsum et tortor ornare ullamcorper nec quis orci.
- Suspendisse nec urna sit amet arcu volutpat imperdiet vitae et velit.
- Donec et ipsum interdum, vulputate augue eu, aliquam ipsum.
- Integer sed turpis tempus sem laoreet pellentesque vitae tincidunt
- Maecenas mattis mauris non neque fermen
  dignissim.
- Aliq

employers, projects, professional achievements, educational institutions, volunteer efforts, clubs, hobbies, and any other information that portrays a detailed view of the person. The résumé and CV are companion documents, and when viewed together they paint a well-rounded picture of an individual.

It is very important to understand that both a CV and a résumé can and should be customized based on the intended recipient. If a job seeker is applying to multiple jobs at different robotics companies, the résumé and CV will have to be adjusted to make the candidate appear attractive for each particular company and industry.

For instance, imagine a mechanical engineer applying for a job at an aerospace robotics company and a different job at a marine science robotics company. Although the engineering work may be similar at both companies, it is best to make one's CV and résumé appear well suited to the specific qualifications of each industry. The goal is not to mislead or lie. Rather it is to paint the most truthful picture of oneself in order to appear to be the best possible candidate for any given job or opportunity.

EXTRACURRICULAR ACTIVITIES

Although academics are essential, it is very important to be involved with extracurricular activities such as clubs, volunteer work, and more. Participating in a group like the Boy Scouts or Girl Scouts is a great way to learn valuable life skills such as teamwork, discipline, and the value of volunteerism.

Many schools will offer students opportunities to participate in club activities such as debate, computer programming, sports, photography, drama, and other similar programs. Participating in these kinds of clubs and groups helps to make you become a well-rounded individual by exposing you to activities and skills that you would not normally encounter.

Fortunately there are many extracurricular clubs and programs that offer students access to working with robotics and computers. Any student interested in a future in robotics should seek to join and actively participate in as many science and math clubs as possible. Participating in clubs and programs will expose students to advanced and specialized topics, and it will also encourage social interaction between students who are interested in robotics. Having friends who share your interests is a great way to keep motivated and to enhance your learning opportunities.

College entrance boards, the gatekeepers who decide whether or not a student is accepted to a college, often value extracurricular activities listed on a candidate's résumé. Having extracurricular activities listed on one's résumé helps a student to appear as an active, passionate, and curious individual. Colleges want to enroll the best students, and often "best" means something more than grades. They do this to compare the top students. Extracurricular activities can set one student apart from others. Colleges offering robotics degrees often have limited spaces open each year, so they will look to fill those spots with students who have demonstrated the most consistent interest and passion for the field and practice of robotics.

THE QUADCOPTER

The quadcopter has quickly become a very affordable and practical robot for just about anyone to purchase and use. A quadcopter is a remote-controlled helicopter with four rotors that can be operated much like any remote-controlled device. Quadcopters also have GPS chips, logic boards, and flight controllers that make flying the device totally autonomous. The operator can preprogram multiple waypoints for a single flight and set the quadcopter loose. Using GPS, the quadcopter can fly to those predetermined waypoints and then return back to its initial takeoff location without any additional human interaction.

Quadcopter flight controllers have become so precise and effective that it is now feasible to mount small video cameras on them for professional filming. Adventure enthusiasts have been using quadcopters to capture footage of rock climbing, skiing, and surfing, among other sports. Recently major Hollywood film studios have discovered how effective and affordable quadcopter cameras can be and have begun using them in production of major films.

MENTORSHIPS AND INTERNSHIPS

Mentors are people whom students and professionals seek out to provide guidance, encouragement, and inspiration. Mentors can be anyone as long as they are willing to put in the time and effort required to provide a meaningful experience for the mentee. A mentor can be an older student, a relative, a teacher, or a professional. The primary purpose of a mentorship is for the mentee to see how the mentor behaves and performs in order to pattern his or her own behavior and performance in a similar way.

Professional mentorships involve a seasoned professional providing a young person with access to his or her work in the form of projects or shared work. It is very important to choose a mentor who has experience in the field of robotics in which the mentee is interested, as this will ensure a productive and interesting mentorship.

An internship is similar to a mentorship but differs in that the focus of the experience is not one to one; rather it is a limited employment opportunity that is generally done for little or no compensation. Many businesses will sponsor internships, which can be mutually beneficial. The business gets a temporary low-cost worker who may someday become a fully paid employee. The intern gets hands-on experience and training that would not otherwise be available. Internships are great tools to enhance a résumé, and colleges and recruiters look very favorably upon them.

In the case of both mentorships and internships, it is important to find opportunities that provide you with experience and expertise. This experience may come from mentors or companies that have both the capability and the time to devote to the mentee or intern. Furthermore it is critical that the mentorship or internship be with individuals or companies engaged in the business of robotics.

COLLEGE PREPARATION

Preparing for college is something that should start on the first day of freshmen year of high school. The enrollment requirements and standards set by most colleges are increasingly strict, and it is becoming more difficult for students to find placements at schools. Because of these increasing hurdles, it is very important for a young student to begin building a strong academic record, preparing for college board tests, and building a rounded résumé early.

This recommendation for preparation may seem obvious, but students often wait until it is too late to craft an academic career that will enable them to pursue their top-tier school picks. Students seeking enrollment into a robotics collegiate program should focus their studies on math, physics, computer programming, electronics, and mechanical assembly. Participation in after-school programs and clubs dedicated to robotics and science will be a big plus.

In your first interview, you will be evaluated on how well you can describe who you are, what you've accomplished, and how you can use your talents.

INFORMATIONAL INTERVIEWS

Informational interviews are short one-on-one meetings in which a prospective student or job applicant seeks to interview a professional or expert about a particular topic. Some informational interviews may be with a company executive in order to learn more about that company or about the industry in which that company operates. It is also possible to request an informational interview of a professor at a university or college that a student may want to attend.

The goal of the informational interview is to learn about the job. There is another benefit of showing the interviewer that you are motivated and inquisitive. Many doors can be opened through the process of seeking an informational interview. Students who want careers working with robotics should seek to interview current professionals who work in the field to learn as much as they can about the work and the life the career affords. Finding a professional in robotics to interview will require some research on the Internet. The companies who work with NASA or DARPA are a great place to start your search.

SUMMER JOBS

Having a summer job or part-time job during the school year is a great way to earn some money and also to learn some valuable skills. Student who can successfully hold a summer job prove to others that they are productive and reliable.

A summer job may seem like a small thing, but there are many young people who do not have the patience, dedication, or interest in taking a summer job. By showing that you can work and uphold the bargain between employee and employer, you are proving yourself to be a loyal and trustworthy team player.

For the student looking for a career in robotics, it would be best to look for a summer job that will expose the student to robotics, mechanical systems, electronics, or basic science. Getting as much exposure to scientific activity and science professionals as possible will give students greater understanding of the work they can expect to do when they begin their professional career.

HOBBIES

In life it is important to have hobbies and interests that are unrelated to your school or professional work. For those folks who choose to pursue education and work in a field that interests them personally, they get the benefit of being passionate about their work and their hobbies. Today it is quite easy to have a passion for robotics and develop a very satisfying hobby in the field.

The parts, tools, and skills needed to be a hobby roboticist are readily available to anyone with the interest and passion to pursue it. There are thousands of free and low-cost robotics projects that can be found online. There are hundreds of robotics clubs and groups that meet around the country to have fun and network.

Having a hobby that lines up with your educational and career goals is great because you will be learning things in your target field just by having fun! The aspiring roboticist should seek hobbies like flying drone copters, assembling remote-controlled cars, creating robotic toys, building robotics kits, and working with computer hardware and software.

CHAPTER SEVEN

THE FUTURE!

The future of robotics is wide open to any idea one can envision. There are countless applications of robotics that improve life or are simply fun. The developments in robotics that we have seen to date are only a glimpse of what is possible. The only limitation that exists to stifle the pace of development in robotics is the potential for a lack of qualified and capable students to pick up the efforts of the current work force.

ROBOTS TO THE RESCUE

Currently in development and likely to be put into service in the not-too-distant future are robots designed specifically to perform search and rescue in hazardous environments. Humans are physically vulnerable to many environmental variables such as heat, cold, atmospheric pressure, and radiation. Machines are generally not susceptible to such hazards assuming they are designed to withstand them.

In some disaster areas, the environment may be too hazardous to rescue workers to allow them to access stranded victims. This limitation is being addressed with the creation of search-and-rescue robots. There are many designs being tested by many different companies. The general principle is the same in each case, though: building a robot that can remotely or autonomously enter a hazardous area, find survivors, and then extract them to a safe location. Robots can have sensory equipment and physical capabilities that far exceed that of a human, which allows them to search more effectively than a human could. Robots can also have the capability to perform physical tasks that a human could not, such as carrying multiple injured people simultaneously.

In some cases the robotics involved in the process of search and rescue are no more complex than a

Robots will increasingly be used on the battlefield to reduce the risk to soldiers and to perform tasks that can save the injured.

simple remote drone, which can fly over a disaster area to visually locate hazards and survivors. In 2013 in New York City, two buildings exploded due to an underground gas leak. Following the explosion, the flames, heat, and unstable structures made it impossible for firefighters to search for survivors. A civilian who lived near the site of the explosion owned a quadcopter drone with a remote control and camera. He flew his drone over and through the disaster site and was able to deliver video footage to the firefighters on the scene showing where survivors were located and where fires were burning. This simple drone with a camera saved lives.

ROBOTS IN MEDICINE

Robots in the field of medicine are changing the delivery of medical treatments at an ever-increasing pace. The types of surgeries and procedures that can be performed by robotic devices are more precise and more repeatable than any human surgeon could ever perform.

Today, eye surgeons are able to reshape the surface of a cornea and the shape of a lens in order to improve and restore vision without ever having to

A doctor uses a robot to perform a highly complex surgical process. Robots are extremely precise, which enables surgeries on very small and delicate tissue.

cut the eye of the patient. Bladeless laser procedures have been performed for over a decade now, and the new equipment in place is substantially more precise, resulting in a nearly 100 percent success rate.

ROBOTS IN THE MILITARY

Bomb disposal robots were first introduced in the early 2000s by the United States during the Iraq and Afghanistan wars. In both wars, enemy combatants used mines and explosives against U.S. troops and as a result caused many casualties. The U.S. Department of Defense contracted multiple companies to build remotely controlled disposal robots that could be controlled by a disposal specialist from a safe distance away from the explosive device.

Several different types of robots were developed. Some disposal robots were quite small and were carried on the back of a disposal specialist like a heavy backpack. These small robots enabled quick response and rapid deployment to locations where bombs were discovered.

Other disposal robots were much larger and would serve to address larger types of bombs that required more tools and appendages to disarm. In either case these robots served to save lives by defusing active bombs safely or, in the case of an unintentional detonation, saved the life of the disposal specialist operating the robot.

Brain surgeons are able to perform very delicate and complex brain surgeries using minimally invasive techniques. By reducing the amount of exposure to air and other contaminants, the risk of infection drops dramatically. Additionally, because of the perfection of movement made by robotic surgical devices there is very little chance of unintended surgical mistakes.

As robots are made smaller and smaller, we will approach the era of autonomous internal robots. Miniature robots will be injected into the body for delivering medicine and performing microscopic surgeries from the inside of the body without needing the body to be opened by a surgeon.

TRANSPORTATION

In the very near future we will begin to see a new generation of automobiles sold to the public that will incorporate self-driving features. Car manufacturers are racing to be the first to sell completely driverless cars, and they are getting assistance from the federal government. The U.S. Department of Transportation is actively sponsoring research and development into the area of smart cars and smart highways.

The goal of smart cars, smart roads, and driverless cars is to remove human error from the process of driving. Most car accidents are the result of poor driver decisions, drunk driving, or pure accident. Humans are not as good at driving safely as are robotic cars. The goal is to reduce the number

Researchers are working on robotic assistive devices for the automobile industry to help reduce the incidence of accidents and traffic.

of accidents by connecting cars and roads via communications systems so that information about road conditions and other cars can be used for safer transportation.

In addition to automobiles, the aviation industry is also in the midst of major transformation as the capabilities of drones and self-piloted vehicles increase. The near future will bring autonomous drones that deliver goods quickly, such as an organ for a human transplant or medical supplies for disaster victims. We already see many drones in use in the military and are likely to see our local police and firefighters begin to rapidly adopt drones and robots to assist with their daily work to safeguard the population from harm.

Companies in the oil and gas industry are using robots to map and explore the sea floor in order to discover new oil and gas reserves that can be drilled and tapped. Geologists are using drones to explore volcanoes where heat and poison gases would kill any person.

A final note worth considering is that robots are here to stay. As you plan your life and career, you can very easily find your way into some aspect of the field of robotics. The only question you need to answer is, "Which field of robotics should I enter?" The future will bring us incredible advances in robotics and will enable humanity to further its knowledge of the universe and improve the quality of our lives.

If you need one final note to further excite you about robotics, it's important to keep in mind that as far as we know our moon is the only one in the entire galaxy that is entirely populated by robots. Several nations have active robotic projects on the moon, all with the goal of better understanding the geologic nature of our closest neighbor.

GLOSSARY

actuator A motor that provides any and all kinds of movements in a robotic device. An actuator can be a motor to push a wheel, to move a mechanical arm, or to focus an optical lens.

aesthetic The beauty or art of something. In robotics applying aesthetics to a robot would be to make it attractive or beautiful to behold.

articulation In robotics, the ability of appendages (arms or legs) to move around an axis.

autonomous Describes a robotic device that is able to move and act independent of human input for the performance of a task or set of tasks. An example of an autonomous robot is the iRobot Roomba that vacuums without a person needing to direct it.

complementary Describes any object or action that enhances another object or action.

computer science The study of computer code, computer machine language, and computational theory for the development and expansion of the body of knowledge about computers. Computer scientists look for ways to improve computer performance and capability.

esoteric Relating to topics or theories that are very specialized and understood by a very small group of people.

innate Having a strong skill for something like mathematics or computer programming; having a natural talent.

multidisciplinary Requiring the study of more than one discipline because of their innate complexity.

pneumatics Mechanical devices that use air compression to move pistons inside of tubes.

servo A motor most commonly used for the manipulation of robotic appendages. The Atlas robot has servos at its elbows that actuate movement just like that of a human elbow.

FOR MORE INFORMATION

Canadian Space Agency
John H. Chapman Space Centre
6767 Route de l'Aéroport
Saint-Hubert, QB J3Y 8Y9
Canada
(450) 926-4800
Web site: http://www.asc-csa.gc.ca/eng
The Canadian Space Agency is the Canadian
counterpart to NASA. Its goal is to lead the
development and application of space knowledge for
the benefit of Canadians and humanity. The CSA is
involved with the International Space Station and is
designing and deploying new robotic rovers annually.

DARPA
675 North Randolph Street
Arlington, VA 22203-2114
(703) 526-6630
Web site: http://www.darpa.mil
DARPA is the science research and development arm of
the U.S. Defense Department. DARPA is responsible
for numerous R&D projects in the area of robotics. The
autonomous car challenge and the Robotics Challenge
are two of the projects under DARPA that involve
collaboration between DARPA, private companies,
and universities. DARPA's efforts at advancing
science and technology have greatly impacted the
technological capabilities of the nation through the
invention of breakthrough technologies such as the
Internet, which it began working on in the 1950s.

NASA
Suite 5R30
Washington, DC 20546
(202) 358-0001
Web site: http://www.nasa.gov
NASA was created by the National Aeronautics and
Space Act of 1958. NASA has been tasked with
furthering the technical knowledge, capability, and
resources of the United States in the areas of science
and technology and space exploration. NASA has
been one of the greatest contributors to robotics
research and development. Currently NASA has plans
to send more robots to the surface of Mars.

U.S. Department of Education
400 Maryland Avenue SW
Washington, DC 20202
(800) 872-5327
Web site: http://www.ed.gov
The U.S. Deptartment of Education oversees U.S.
education standards and practices and ensures that
states have adequate funding to pay for their students'
educations and that the standards of education are at
a level consistent with the productive needs of society.

WEBSITES

Because of the changing nature of Internet links, Ros-
en Publishing has developed an online list of websites
related to the subject of this book. This site is updated
regularly. Please use this link to access the list:

http://www.rosenlinks.com/PTC/Robot

FOR FURTHER READING

Baichtel, John. *Basic Robot Building with LEGO Mindstorms NXT 2.0.* Indianapolis, IN: Que Publishing, 2013.

Benedettelli, Daniele. *The LEGO Mindstorms EV3 Laboratory: Build, Program, and Experiment with Five Wicked Cool Robots!* San Francisco, CA: No Starch Press, 2013.

Cantor, Doug. *The Big Book of Hacks: 264 Amazing DIY Tech Projects.* San Francisco, CA: Weldon Owen, 2012.

Ceceri, Kathy. *Robotics: Discover the Science and Technology of the Future with 20 Projects* (Build It Yourself). White River Junction, VT: Nomad Press, 2012.

Donat, Wolfram. *Make a Raspberry Pi-Controlled Robot: Building a Rover with Python, Linux, Motors, and Sensors.* San Francisco, CA: Maker Media, Inc., 2014.

Fiske, Edward. *Fiske Guide to Colleges 2015.* Naperville, IL: Sourcebooks, 2014.

Hackett, Chris. *The Big Book of Maker Skills (Popular Science): 334 Tools & Techniques for Building Great Tech Projects.* San Francisco, CA: Weldon Owen, 2014.

Karvinen, Tero, Kimmo Karvinen, and Ville Valtokari. *Make: Sensors: A Hands-On Primer for Monitoring the Real World with Arduino and Raspberry Pi.* Sebastopol, CA: Maker Media, Inc., 2014.

McComb, Gordon. *Robot Builder's Bonanza.* Fourth edition. New York, NY: McGraw-Hill/TAB Electronics, 2012.

Peterson's. *Four-Year Colleges 2015* (Peterson's Four Year Colleges). New York, NY: Peterson's, 2014.

Peterson's. *Teens' Guide to College & Career Planning.* New York, NY: Peterson's, 2014.

Platt, Charles. *Make: Electronics* (Learning by Discovery). Sebastopol, CA: Maker Media, Inc., 2009.

Princeton Review. *The Complete Book of Colleges.* 2015 edition (College Admissions Guides). Cambridge, MA: Princeton Review, 2014.

Salemi, Behnam. *Robot Building for Teens.* Boston, MA: Cengage Learning, 2015.

Shulman, Mark. *TIME for Kids Explorers: Robots.* New York, NY: Time for Kids Explorers, 2014.

BIBLIOGRAPHY

Discovery Education. *Discovery Education STEM Careers for Students* (DVD Set). New York, NY: Discovery Education, 2010.

Fardo, Stephen, James Masterson, and Larry Ross. *Robotics: Theory and Industrial Applications.* Tinley Park, IL: Goodheart-Wilcox, 2010.

Honey, Margaret, and David E. Kanter. *Design, Make, Play: Growing the Next Generation of STEM Innovators.* New York, NY: Routledge, 2013.

Kupperburg, Paul. *Careers in Robotics.* London, England: Read How You Want, 2012.

Neumeier, Marty. *Metaskills: Five Talents for the Robotic Age.* San Francisco, CA: New Riders, 2012.

Newport, Cal. *How to Be a High School Superstar: A Revolutionary Plan to Get into College by Standing Out (Without Burning Out).* New York, NY: Three Rivers Press, 2010.

Payment, Simone. *Robotics Careers: Preparing for the Future.* New York, NY: Rosen Central, 2011.

Shulman, Mark. *TIME for Kids Explorers: Robots.* New York, NY: Time for Kids Explorers, 2014.

Siegwart, Roland, and Reza Norbakhsh. *Introduction to Autonomous Mobile Robots* (Intelligent Robotics and Autonomous Agents). Cambridge, MA: The MIT Press, 2011.

Springer, Sally P., Jon Reider, Joyce Vining Morgan. *Admission Matters: What Students and Parents Need to Know About Getting into College*. New York, NY: Jossey-Bass, 2013.
Stewart, Melissa. *National Geographic Readers: Robots*. New York, NY: National Geographic Children's Books, 2014.

INDEX

ABOUT THE AUTHOR

Peter Ryan works in the IT and publishing industries. He has worked on many technical IT projects and web-based applications. He has an undergraduate degree from Villanova University and an MBA from Rensselaer Polytechnic Institute. He has worked in high-tech environments in various roles and has spent several years working in the video game industry in product development and sales.

PHOTO CREDITS